The Princess and the Valley Man

Luna's and Solis adventures in Death Valley

Dorota Kluza & Evan Williams

III Clink Street

London | New York

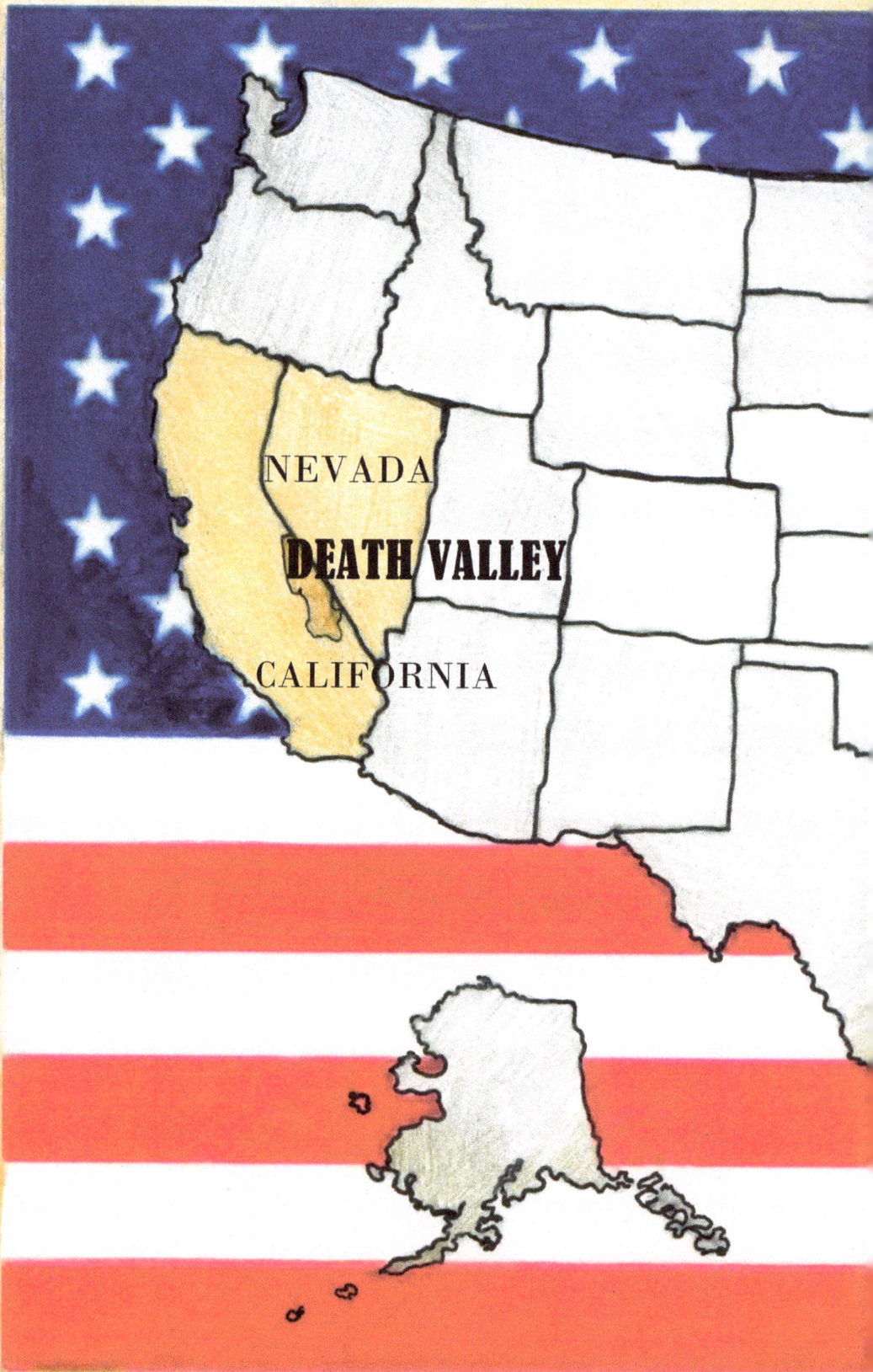

NEVADA

DEATH VALLEY

CALIFORNIA

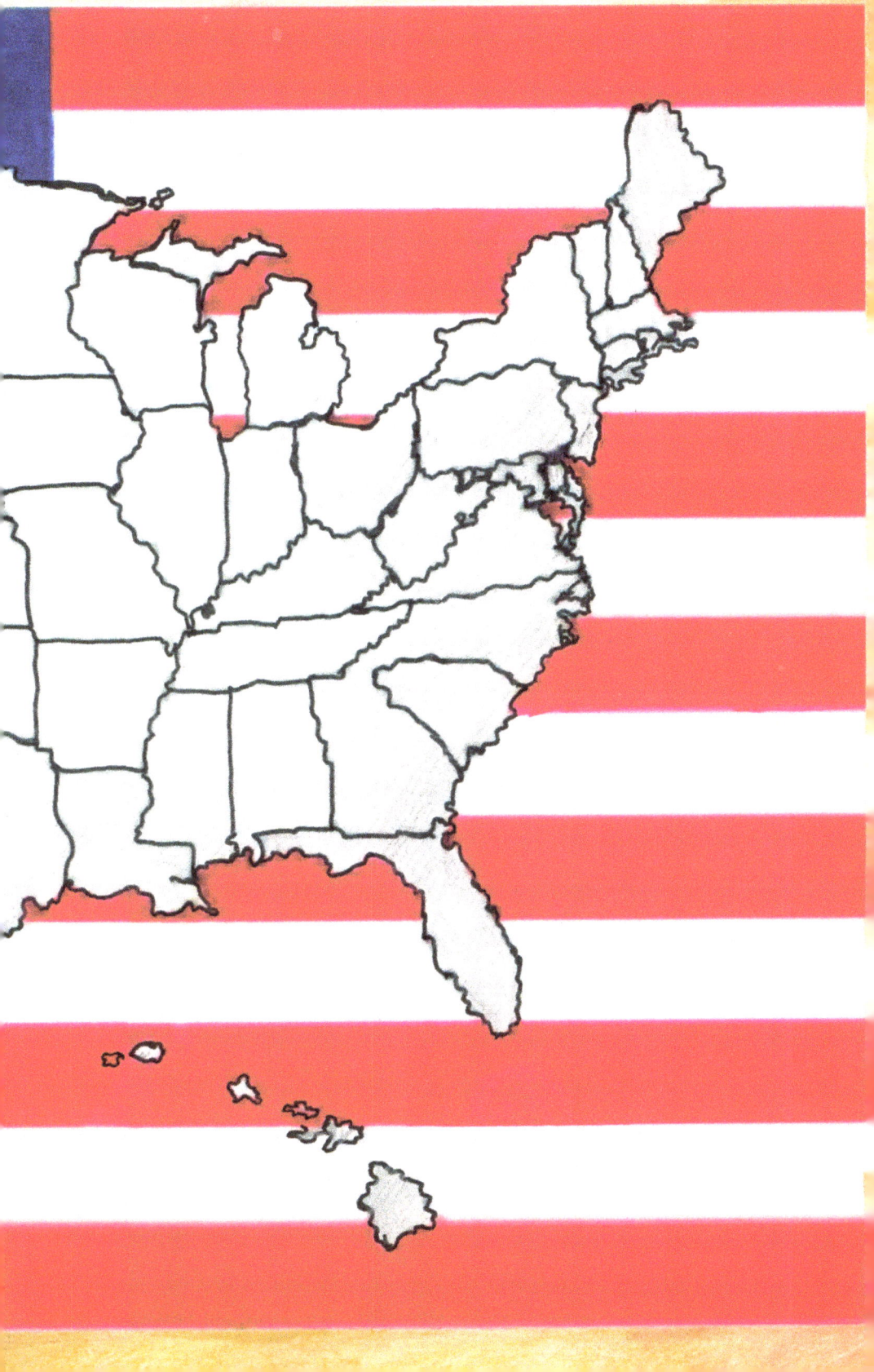

Published by Clink Street Publishing 2018

Copyright © 2018

First edition.

ISBN:
978-1-913340-31-5 - paperback
978-1-913340-32-2 - ebook

Dedication

"Very special thank you to my wonderful parents
Bogumiła Hilak-Kluza and Bolesław Kluza for showing me
the world of imagination and fantasy which taught me
that anything is possible."

— *Dorota Kluza*

"Thank you to my parents KC and Gene Williams for
always supporting me in my goals and giving me
the inspiration to achieve them."

— *Evan Williams*

Introduction

Join Solis and Luna as they travel through America's most breathtaking and beautiful natural environments, the National Parks. In this series of books, Solis and Luna embark on boundless amazing adventures, make new friends, and learn about wildlife, ecology, and the history of the National Parks with a twist of fantasy mixed in on their mystic journeys.

This series of books, *The Princess and The Valley Man*, aims to teach children about the importance of nature and wildlife and these truly unique places that we all get to share called the National Parks. Through Solis and Luna's adventures in our National Parks, children will be able to learn about the unique features of each place they visit and enjoy the journey.

Table of Contents

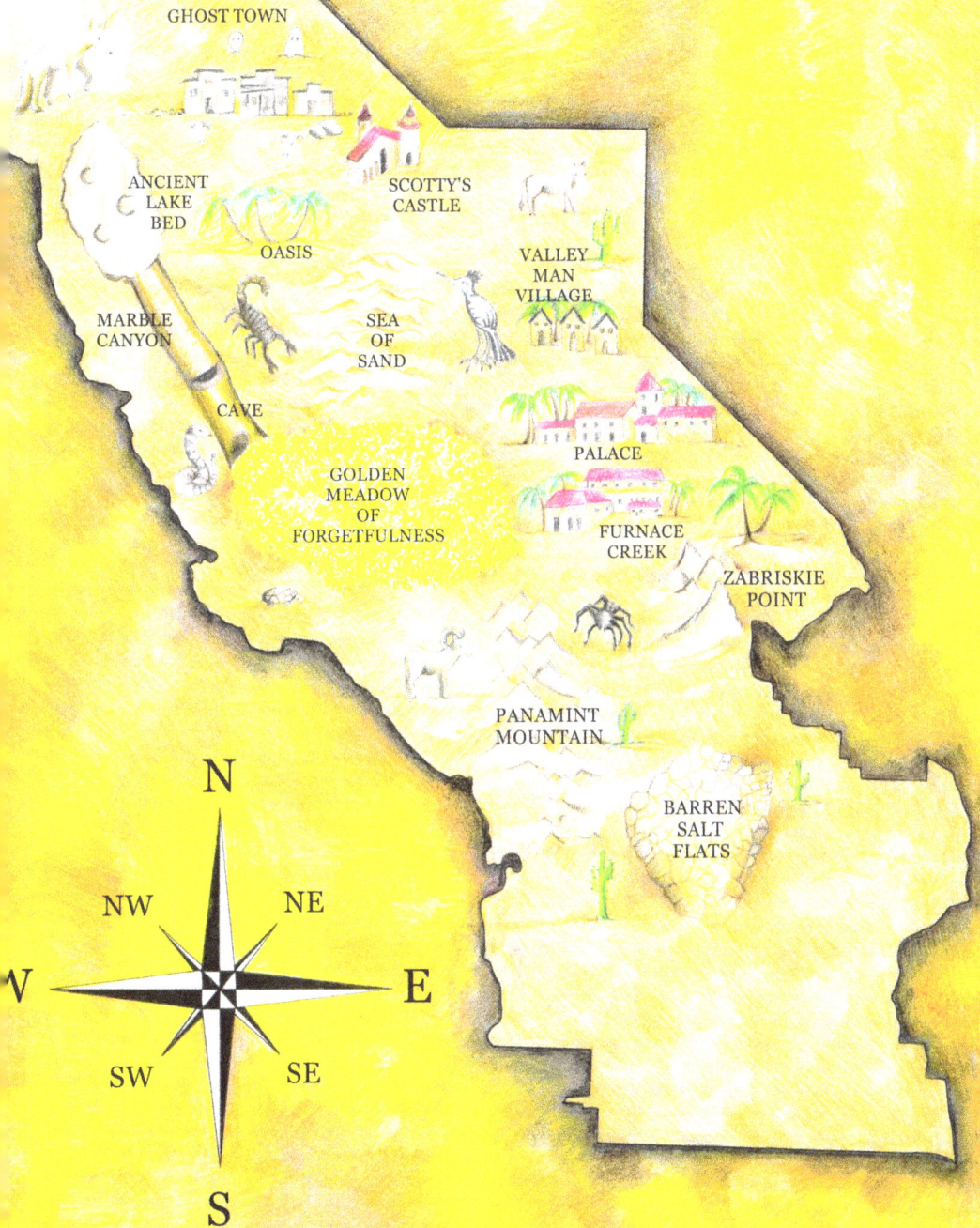

DEATH VALLEY
NATIONAL PARK

GHOST TOWN

ANCIENT
LAKE
BED

OASIS

SCOTTY'S
CASTLE

VALLEY
MAN
VILLAGE

MARBLE
CANYON

SEA
OF
SAND

CAVE

PALACE

GOLDEN
MEADOW
OF
FORGETFULNESS

FURNACE
CREEK

ZABRISKIE
POINT

PANAMINT
MOUNTAIN

BARREN
SALT
FLATS

N

NW   NE

W   E

SW   SE

S

Chapter 1
The Sand Beast

There was a place on Earth that was considered most unusual: Death Valley, which was in California in the United States. Now you might be asking yourself: what make's Death Valley so unusual? Well, it was a land of extremes. While it had towering mountains, it also had below-sea-level salt flats and even sand dunes. All strewn across the landscape were rock formations of many colors, some of which held mystery. Sometimes, when the rain comes at the right time, the landscape would bloom with an explosion of flowers. These mostly grow from the many seeds that had been waiting in the dirt; sometimes they wait many years for the rain to come. Mostly, though, it is the heat that makes this place famous. You see, Death Valley is the hottest place on Earth!

One day, because of Death Valley's unique terrain and features that focused the sun's energy upon itself, it reached a temperature of 134 degrees Fahrenheit (56,6 Celsius degrees) - the hottest temperature ever recorded on Earth. Something very special also happened on that day: a child was born in this place of extremes. This child, some say, got something even more special from the sun on that day, an inexplicable kind of energy that would be with him wherever he went which kept him safe and protected him from harm. His parents called him Solis. He was an extraordinary boy who grew up in this most interesting and unusual place. He was not afraid of anything and he made lots of friends, including local animals that he used to play with. A born explorer who never gets sick, decided one day to take it upon himself to protect and preserve Death Valley, which he loved with all his heart.

As a young man, Solis travelled to many places far and wide and has seen many kingdoms. In fact, as a former soldier in his kingdom's army, he had fought in many battles. His exploits were famous throughout the lands, especially among schoolchildren who were studying history. Living in Death Valley, he worked by helping those who came to seek adventure and see the amazing sights.

One day, on his way back home after a deeply exhausting day at work, he came upon a group of travelers who had become trapped in their big coach within a massive sand cloud. He sped up his wagon to reach them quickly and to help them get out of it. He knew it was not a typical sand cloud caused by the wind, but a monstrous attack of a deadly sand creature living in this area that could not stand any noise. Luckily for the travellers, Solis was not afraid of it!

"Do not leave your coach!" Solis screamed. "Close the windows and your doors, and be as quiet as possible!"

But the travellers were overwhelmed with fear and panic. "Help us and get us out of here!" They screamed. "Get us out of here, please!"

Solis jumped off his wagon as quickly as he could. He looked like a cowboy wearing an old Western-looking bandana on his face and a special pair of shoes designed to not sink on any surface. He ran to them, then tied a big thick cotton rope from his wagon to their coach. But at this moment, the scary sand creature came out of the sand cloud and started to shake the noisy coach violently from one side to the other.

The travellers were screaming loudly from fear, but Solis was not afraid of the creature at all. He stayed calm, carefully connecting the rope. He made a few quick steps, like he was floating on the sand on his wide flat shoes, and was back in his wagon in a second, pulling the tourists and their coach away from this dangerous sand monster.

Once they all were on safe ground, Solis emerged from his wagon covered in sand. "Are you all okay? Is anyone hurt?" His voice was calm, reassuring. "This was the sand beast living in this area. I hope she did not scare you too much. Next time you must be more careful here and must follow some precautions. By the way, my name is Solis."

Just as he introduced himself to the travellers, he saw among them the most beautiful girl he had ever seen. He was entranced. But the travellers interrupted his reverie, crying with happiness and saying, "You saved us! You saved us! Thank you so much, Solis!"

"Oh my goodness, you are all covered in sand," one of them said, helping Solis dust the dirt off his shirt. "We are very sorry for this trouble, but we got confused by the intense heat of this place. Luckily, we found the coach. But when we tried to drive out, the beast attacked us. You know the rest of the story, Solis. You are our hero!"

Solis's face blushed from the attention. "Oh, I'm not a hero, guys. I am just glad I could help and to make sure you are all fine. Travellers often get confused from the heat here. Ordinary folks could rarely stand the kind of heat we have in Death Valley. Just be more careful next time, wear a hat and drink lots of water, and watch out and take precautions to avoid the sand beasts in this area." Solis flashed them a smile that was pure charm.

"We would love to thank you, somehow, Solis," said someone from the group. "Please allow us to invite you for dinner tonight?"

"It is really not necessary," he replied, but then he could not take his eyes off the beautiful girl. "But of course, I would love to have dinner with you all."

"Hoooraay!" they cheered in unison. "See you tonight at the Last Kind Words Saloon?"

"See you then," replied Solis happily.

On the way to their accommodation, the travellers could not stop talking about how Solis fought off the deadly sand creature, and how brave he was for saving them. And among them, the beautiful girl that Solis liked merely smiled, quietly anticipating to meet him again.

Chapter 2
The Beautiful Princess

When the evening came they all met in the Last Kind Words Saloon, except for the girl that Solis was hoping to meet that night.

"Sorry, but one of our friends could not join us tonight," the group told Solis. "Her name is Luna and she did not feel too well from the incident today with the sand beast. She is sensitive to rapid movements. Luna is also our very dear friend from a distant place. You would never believe it, but she comes from a star kingdom and she is a princess! But please tell us about yourself and your life here in Death Valley."

Solis' heart sank upon hearing that Luna would not be joining them. Nevertheless, he started to tell his story to the travellers quite enthusiastically, hoping to see Luna another time.

"The Death Valley I live in is a place of extremes as you probably noticed today. It is hot and dry and may seem lifeless, yet it is home to many types of plants and animals and it can be full of wonder and beauty at times. Death Valley is both dangerous and majestic, and for these reasons people often come to visit just like you did."

The travellers were so surprised with what Solis said, even more so that he was able to live in this place. "But how can you live here with such extreme conditions?"

"I am not just a typical valley man," Solis replied. "I travelled to many places far and wide and seen many kingdoms from many different tribes. I was also a part of my kingdom's army and fought in many battles. I have been educated in many fields of study. Now, I live here in Death Valley and enjoy the rawness of nature and the harsh lessons of surviving against the odds."

"Wow! That sounds unbelievable. We do not think we could do it," they all agreed, laughing good-naturedly. They then told Solis that they had come here for a short honeymoon because two of them just got married in the kingdom not too far from here.

"We are planning to explore the majestic sights in Death Valley, relax here and take amazing wedding pictures amid these breathtakingly beautiful surroundings," they explained.

"Congratulations," said Solis. "I am sure you will have an incredible time with unforgettable memories from Death Valley."

They talked avidly deep into the night. By the time the clock struck twelve, they were all tired from the events of the day and said goodnight to one another.

While helping a different group of travellers the following day, Solis noticed the beautiful Luna coming into the cabin where he was working. He did not expect to meet her there at all. Solis' heart raced as Luna approached him.

"Hi Luna, how are you feeling today? I missed you at the dinner last night," said Solis, wondering why he was able to be so direct because he was usually shy. Luna looked at him strangely.

"You don't recognize me, do you?" Solis laughed. "No wonder, I had a bandana on my face and looked like a sand mummy when we first met."

Luna also laughed, but nervously. "Oh, hi, Solis. It's true I did not recognize you. You look very different today and your eyes are amazingly blue." Luna gazed fondly into those magnetic eyes.

"Yes, I did not feel well enough to go out last night. I had been shaken too much, I guess. My stomach felt like being upside down." And then they both laughed loudly again.

"By the way, I have not had a chance to introduce myself to you, yet. My name is Luna, but you know it already. Thank you again for saving us yesterday."

"Of course, I could not possibly do it any other way," Solis beamed. "Your friends told me you are Princess Luna."

"Hmmmm… I do not quite like to introduce myself using my royal status. I am just Luna. I came to get a map of Death Valley and some information about places to visit here. Could you please help me with it? You sure do live in a spectacular part of the world," she said.

Solis was very happy to listen to her and was absolutely mesmerized by her softly spoken voice. "Of course, Luna. I am glad to help and explain everything. I'll show you a map of the best places to visit in Death Valley. I also suggest you check out our exposition for visitors about Death Valley in the cabin before you leave."

Solis nodded and smiled, until she moved away and continued to browse around his cabin.

When she was leaving, she turned to Solis and gave him a warm sweet smile, which made Solis's heart leap for joy. *She's the most beautiful woman I have ever seen*, Solis thought to himself. Yet he was so smitten he said nothing.

Solis' heart pounded in his chest. He knew he wouldn't be able to forget her.

The next day, while guiding a group of travellers out to the barren salt lands, Solis noticed a small group of people who seemed dressed rather unusually for this occasion. There was a couple who were in wedding clothes, and several other people with them. Then Solis remembered the conversation he had at dinner with the travellers who he saved from the sand creature. They said during the dinner that they want to take some wedding pictures here.

At this point, he was almost finished with his tour, so he decided to go and have a better look at what was happening. He saw that the beautiful girl from the day before was among them. His heart leapt with joy. Suddenly feeling overwhelmingly shy, Solis slowly approached her, his heart racing and he felt like running away, right before she turned to him and gave him a warm welcoming smile.

Feeling braver, Solis smiled back at her. "Hi everyone. I see you've found a great spot for pictures."

"Yes, we absolutely love it here," they all replied. And then Luna chimed in quite sweetly. "It is so beautiful here. Solis, you are quite lucky to live here." She smiled.

"I'm so glad to be here," she chirped. "Can you tell me more about this place? This is so interesting."

"Well," Solis began. He was only too glad to be of service. He began telling her about what he knew about Death Valley, and what it was like to live there in the middle of what seemed like an arid landscape.

"It's not at all arid." They smiled at each other as they walked back to the carriages.

"Would you like to see me again?" Solis asked. "Let's meet up tonight at the Last Kind Words Saloon?"

"I'd love to," she said, her eyes twinkling with anticipation.

Solis finished his work for the day with nothing on his mind but the beautiful Princess Luna. He could not wait to see her again, so much that when she finally showed up at the Last Kind Words Saloon's doorstep, his heart raced and he felt so happy.

Luna noticed several portraits hanging on the wall behind the bar. "Who are all these men in the paintings?" She asked. "A lot of them look like you, except they all have funny handlebar mustaches and you don't." They both chuckled.

"These are our past valley men," Solis explained. "They are the founding fathers of Death Valley but only one of them is actually my relative. This guy here was my great grandfather Helios. He was a great valley man. I never got to meet him, however, as he vanished one day while out looking for lost visitors."

"I did not realize that your family had such a past with living in Death Valley," replied Luna.

"They are still many things we do not know about each other but hopefully we get a chance to become better friends in the future," replied Solis smiling innocently.

That night at the saloon, Solis and Luna had many laughs and talked the night away. It was all perfect until Princess Luna asked the question: "So what exciting things shall we do tomorrow?"

Chapter 3
The New Year's Eve Party

The next day was a special day - the changing of the year. Princess Luna was with her friends touring the Sea of Sand and the Mosaic Canyon, which are both very beautiful and popular sights in Death Valley.

Solis finished his work earlier than usual so that he could get ready for the party that the valley men held to celebrate the changing of the year. At the party, Solis could only think of one thing, Princess Luna, who was at the fancy dinner ball in the palace that had been built in Death Valley for its notable visitors.

Yet, the party of the valley men was not even halfway through when a messenger arrived, bearing a note for Solis. "Would you like to join me and my friends at this fabulous ball in the palace?" It was written in a beautiful cursive, signed by Princess Luna. Solis was ecstatic. He rushed to the palace and arrived just on time to join Princess Luna and her friends for the New Year's dinner and dance.

It was a wonderful feast. The local Native American tribe called the Timbisha Shoshone had decided to share their culture and stories with the visitors. They shared some of their traditional dances to welcome the new year and to bring prosperity and good fortune to the people here. They also told stories about Death Valley and the creation of this unusual place.

"I am so hungry," Luna said at one point. "Solis, what is this wonderful dish that the Timbisha made for us?"

"It is called an Indian taco," Solis said. It is a special fried bread with meat, beans, lettuce, tomatoes, and cheese."

"I've never eaten anything like it. It is absolutely delicious. Can I have another one? I think this is my new favorite food," said Luna.

"I am sure that would be fine. They are my favorite thing to eat, too," replied Solis.

Everyone was so excited to learn about the history of Timbisha and get to experience a little bit of their culture and cuisine.

"Solis what can you tell me about the Timbisha," Luna asked.

"Well, Luna, the Timbisha have lived here in Death Valley for more than a thousand years," Solis began. "They get all that they need to live off the land. There are many sacred places here for them so this area is very important to the Timbisha. In fact, the name Timbisha means 'painted rock' and they get that name from the very red colored rock that we have in some areas of this valley."

"Wow, these people are so amazing and have such an extraordinary way of life," Luna exclaimed. "I really enjoyed learning about them and getting to share in some of their culture."

"They are really a great people and there is still a lot we have to learn from them, but this will all take time," said Solis.

Princess Luna and all of her friends had a lot of questions for Solis about being a valley man, and as the evening went

on they all had a wonderful time getting to know each other. When the dinner was over, they went to the ballroom for the dance.

It was a long-standing tradition that when the New Year turns, you get to kiss your dancing partner. Solis was really looking forward to it because he was here with the princess and he really wanted this kiss. After dancing, everyone was given a special drink made from the juice of mesquite beans. It was sweet and had a hint of cinnamon. The Timbisha Shoshone often prepared this drink for special occasions, and tonight they all got this special drink for the toast to welcome in the new year. The countdown started, yet when the clock finally struck twelve, all Solis got was a hug. Princess Luna embraced him, and he stood there not knowing how to return the hug or should he still expect a kiss. But there was nothing else, and when the princess turned to her friends, Solis figured the hug was better than nothing, but it still made him smile.

"Would you like to dance with me one last time?" Solis finally asked the princess. "I have to be at the cabin early tomorrow so I cannot stay too long."

"I would love to," the princess said.

So they danced, and danced, and danced. *This is the happiest night of my life*, Solis thought with the princess in his arms.

But like all good things, the dance had to end. Regardless of what Solis felt, he had to say goodbye, at least for the night. But just before he was supposed to leave the ballroom, a strong wind swept in through the windows, blowing away the curtains to reveal the most amazing spectacle Solis had ever seen: the full moon in all its majesty.

"The moon is amazing," Solis muttered to himself. "I have never seen it so big and bright in my entire life." Luna just smiled to him mysteriously.

The next morning, Solis was still unable to calm down from the previous night's excitement. So, he sent a messenger to the princess to ask her if she could meet him again at the Last Kind Words Saloon in the evening: "Please meet me at the Last Kind Words Saloon in this evening. I would like to show you something".

At the saloon Solis and Luna were having a great time talking. They talked about many things and Solis even told Luna about some of his heroic stories that normally he would not share with anyone.

It was a beautiful night and the sky was clear and full of stars. Solis asked the princess, "It's beautiful out there. Would you like to have a walk by starlight?"

"Maybe," she said. "Where would you like to take me?"

"How about we go to a famous spot over the hill where we could gaze at the stars? It's a bit far and the night's nippy, but it would be all worth it."

Solis was not really expecting her to agree to come with him. After all, it would be some distance. Yet, to his amazement, Princess Luna said, "Yes."

Chapter 4
Zabriskie Point

They got onto his coach and went to Zabriskie Point. This particular spot was a wonderful place all by itself. It was formed by ancient lakes leaving behind different colors of sediment, like chocolate browns, whites, tans, reds, and yellows. Then millions of years of erosion carved the landscape into a masterpiece. Even so, it was an amazing place where two people can watch the stars at night. It was simply breathtaking.

They got out and walked on the small path to the top of the hill. Solis walked on this path many times before and knew his way up the hill but this night was unusually dark despite many shining stars in the sky. It was very difficult to follow the path this time, so Solis took Luna's hand to hold her safely. That moment, Luna's hair started to shine with the millions of stars and made the path brighter and easier to walk on. Solis looked at Luna and did not know what to say at first. Then he told her, "Luna, your hair is glowing like a star! That's amazing." Luna just smiled at him. She was glad it was still quite dark, so Solis could not notice that her cheeks had turned red. She did not like to

show her superpowers but in situations of darkness she could not stop it.

The view of the Milky Way from there was just spectacular, and the stars were shining brighter than ever, much to Solis's amazement. The night, although clear, was rather windy and cold.

"I think it's getting chilly," Princess Luna said.

"Why don't we go back to the coach and watch the stars from there," Solis suggested.

Once they got back at the coach, Solis opened the roof so they could lie down and watch the stars. They stargazed together and Solis was just about to explain to Luna about some of the stars when Luna began to tell him about of the star constellations with a wide knowledge and passion. Solis was very surprised with Luna's knowledge about the name of the stars and all existing star constellations. And he recalled the dinner with her friends again, where they said she comes from the Kingdom of Stars. He also remembered that Luna did not like to be asked about her royal status, and he decided not to ask her any question about it for now.

Suddenly, something unexpected happened: a few shooting stars streaked across the sky, and they began to dance and formed loops and tangents, forming the letters "L" and "S" inside a heart-shaped outline. It was truly magical, and all Solis and Princess Luna could do was laugh and point at the sky and laugh some more. The joy seemed to last for an eternity, and it seemed like no one had ever experienced it before, like it was something special just for them.

Chapter 5
The Sea of Sand

The next day after Solis had finished with his work, he met up with Luna at the Last Kind Words Saloon again and he asked her, "Would you like to go on an adventure with me?"

"Very much so," she replied. Luna couldn't wait to see what he had in mind.

"I will pick you up in a few hours. You will have plenty of time to pack and say good bye to your friends," said Solis.

Luna quickly packed her things and talked to her friends when suddenly she heard a very loud sound. *Beep beep beeeeeep!* She looked out from her window and, to her surprise, there was Solis in a wooden wagon made of some golden shimmering copper elements with funny big wheels and a large white cover over it. The white cover had a honeycomb structure in a geometric pattern.

"Wow, that's an amazing vehicle!" Luna exclaimed. "Where did you get one like that here in Death Valley?"

"Well, building unusual vehicles is my passion. Believe it or not, I built this myself," Solis said. "It has lots of useful ecological solutions and it is reliable in every situation. For example, the white cover is made of flexible solar panels and is lightweight and actually inexpensive to build, and it is powered by the sun's energy! I call my wagon 'Badaboo'."

Luna was deeply impressed. She loved ecological innovations. Solis helped pack Luna's backpack and then they set off together to start their adventure. They got into the Badaboo and started on their way. A short time later, they arrived at their destination. Luna looked around and saw that they were at the Sea of Sand.

"But I have already seen the great sand dunes and the sea of sand," Princess Luna said.

"Not like this," Solis said. "Not how I am about to show you."

When they got out of the Badaboo, Solis pulled two long boards from the trunk of the wagon, one was bright yellow and the other was bright green. The boards were slightly rounded on the front and the edges the back.

Luna looked a little confused and said, "What are we going to do with those?"

"You will see," Solis said. "Just follow me, please. We leave Badaboo here and pick it up later."

Solis and the princess started off on their way to the Sea of Sand with the two boards.

"Where are we going?" Luna asked at one point.

"Do you see the tallest dune out there?"

"Yes," Luna replied.

"Our adventure starts when we get there. But first we have to make it there and it's not going to be easy because from here we need to hike. Vehicles are not allowed off the road in Death Valley. This Sea of Sand may look empty, barren, and void of life but there are fierce and ferocious beasts that live here," said Solis.

Just then, Luna noticed a little kit fox chasing after a kangaroo rat.

"Is this your scary beast?" she said laughing, and all of a sudden she heard a yelp and the kit fox was gone.

"The beast I am talking about lives under the sand," Solis said. "You will not see them until it is too late, but I know the secrets of how to get through this sea of sand without being eaten."

"Oh no," said Luna, "You are talking about the scary sand creature which attacked us!"

"Yes, but do not worry because I know how not to wake them up," replied Solis.

After hiking for several hours, they arrived at the top of the tallest dune and rested.

"I hope all this is going to be worth it," Luna said.

"It will be an adventure unlike any that you have ever had before," Solis said, smiling. "We will see many great and extraordinary things over the next few days, so I hope you are ready for it."

Princess Luna smiled, too, believing him.

After resting for a bit, Solis handed Luna one of the boards.

"What am I going to do with this?" she asked.

"Follow me," Solis said, as he tossed his board on to the downward slope of sand and jumped on to it and started surfing down the dune. Luna followed suit; she discovered she had a natural knack for it.

They did this for hours, surfing down one dune and then climbing up the next and so on.

"This is amazing," said Luna. "It almost feels as though I am flying!"

It began to get dark just as they were at the top of the last dune. The two of them started going down the dune and were having so much fun. Not only was it the last dune, but it was also

the tallest and steepest, which meant they could go really fast. When they were almost to the bottom Luna hit something and flew from her board, rolling and tumbling the rest of the way to the bottom.

Solis rushed to her side. "Are you ok? What happened?"

"I am fine, I am not hurt," she said. "I think my board hit something in the sand. Let's go see what it was." The two of them went back to where Luna fell off and saw that there was something sticking out of the sand. They started digging and discovered a skull. It was not any skull, it was the skull of a Bighorn Sheep.

"What is this?" Luna asked.

"This is the skull of a Bighorn Sheep that lives here. They mostly are in higher places and not very often seen. They like to feed on the plants that live in the mountains and they don't come down here in the valley much."

"Let's make our camp in an oasis that is not far from here," Solis said. "It has everything we need for the night."

Chapter 6

The Kangaroo Rat at the Oasis

When they reached the oasis, Solis gathered some wood from the old dead mesquite trees and started a fire.

"Luna, can you gather some palm leafs and make a sleeping mat for us?" Solis said. "And I will go get us some food."

He quickly set up some traps to catch small game then continued on his search. He came across a palm tree, some of whose dates had fallen. He gathered them all up. Just then he heard his trap go off. He rushed over to it to find a nice plump jackrabbit in it. Solis got the rabbit and the dates and headed back to the fire where Princess Luna was waiting. When he arrived, he saw that the princess had finished the sleeping mats. Then he gathered more wood for the fire because he did not want Luna to be cold at night. Solis did not have to worry about

it because he was always warm no matter the temperature outside.

As they were cooking dinner, Luna noticed that there was a small rodent that was hanging out by the tree.

"Solis, what is that little rodent by the tree over there?" she asked.

Solis looked. "Oh, that would be a kangaroo rat. It is the most impressive animal in Death Valley, I think."

"Really, this little rat," Luna said. "Why?"

"Well, you see, the kangaroo rat does not have to drink or have any water to survive, it is the only animal here that can do that."

"How is this possible?" Luna asked.

"Well, it all started when this place was created," Solis began. "There was a great spirit and he placed all his animals in this amazing lush green tropical forest. There was more than enough food and water for all the animals to be happy. Over time, the climate started to change, and it started to get hotter and dryer. The kangaroo rat noticed this change and started to save water. All the other animals said he was being silly and there was no need for that. Slowly, over time, the streams and rivers started to dry up and the lakes were emptying. The other animals remembered that the kangaroo rat had some water saved, so when they would get thirsty they would just go and ask the kangaroo rat for a drink. The kangaroo rat, being a loyal friend, would always give them some of his water. One day, the kangaroo rat noticed his water supply was getting low and knew that the other animals would be coming for some water, too. The kangaroo rat thought to himself, 'If I give the other animals water, then I won't have any left for me. But they are my friends and I can't just let them go thirsty.' As the day grew hot, the animals showed up asking for water and the kangaroo rat gave it to them. This went on for a few days and each day the kangaroo rat would give all of the other animals his water for that day. One day when it was extremely hot, all the other animals came to get water from the kangaroo rat and being a loyal friend he gave it to them. At the end of the day, he went to get some water for himself and noticed it was all gone. He didn't know what to do and he was just about to cry. Just then he saw a bright light appear in front of him. It was the Great Spirit and he spoke to the kangaroo rat. He said, 'Kangaroo rat, for being such a great and loyal friend and putting the needs of others ahead of your own, I am going to help you. I am going to make sure you never have to worry about drinking water again.' And to this day, the kangaroo rat still does not need to drink any water."

"That is amazing," Luna said. "What an extraordinary animal."

Solis and Luna finished cooking and ate dinner, then just lay back on the mat and watched the stars through the palm trees. The cool desert wind calmly blew through the trees and sand, making that pleasant howl in the night.

"I am getting a little cold," Princess Luna said. Solis pulled her close to him and put his arm around her and cuddled up. And then he asked her: "Is it better now? But he did not get any answer since Luna fell asleep straight away.

"What a wonderful world," Solis thought as they lay there. "I have a beautiful woman at my side, a nice warm fire, an amazing view, and a full belly - what could possibly be better than this? Is it possible for anything to go wrong?"

Yet, as it later turned out, things indeed could go very wrong.

Chapter 7

The Ghost Town

The next day, upon waking up, Solis and Princess Luna saw something that was really amazing: a small town had appeared during the night just on the other side of the oasis, across from where they had camped. How was it possible?

Solis and the princess gathered their things and started to walk toward it. When they got closer, they noticed something most peculiar about this little town. It was hardly more than a dirt road with about a dozen buildings on either side, and they were old and worn down. They looked as though they had not been lived in for over a hundred years or more, some were barely there, and others were just an empty shell. When Solis and Luna stepped out of the oasis and onto the dirt road, a strong gust of wind blew for a brief moment. They started walking down the street and noticed that there was nobody there. Then off in the distance they heard some music. It sounded like a piano playing, and it was coming from one of the old buildings at the end of the road. When they got to the building that had the music,

they saw a sign above the front door that said, "Welcome to the Mad Miner's Saloon! Be gone by sundown or never leave at all."

They looked at each other. Princess Luna said, "I don't think we should go in there."

"Come on, it will be fine," Solis said. "You will see. There is nothing to be afraid of."

When they stepped through the old swinging doors, they saw the piano was playing by itself. At the bar, an old man sat with a drink. He had a long gray beard with mustache, white hair, and his clothes were dirty and tattered. His hat looked as though it had been smashed and had some holes, and he looked like an old gold miner that had been in the mine for far too long.

Solis asked him, "What is the name of this town? I never knew that this place existed, and I have been living here for quite some time now."

But the old man said nothing; he just sat there and took another sip of his drink.

Solis asked again, "Excuse me, what is the name of this place?" Still, only silence from the old man.

Solis started to approach the bar and as he did, the old man finally spoke. "That's quite far enough. This is the town of spirits, the town where the dead do not rest and have no peace. This is a ghost town, and you do not belong here."

Fear clutched Princess Luna's throat. "Can you tell us how to get back home?"

The old man turned, looked at Luna, and said, "You must go to the Land of the Moving Rocks. From there, cross the ancient lake, then go over to the Panamint Mountains. There, you will come across a canyon of marble. Follow this canyon to the end, where you'll find a cave in the rock that was once behind a wall of water. Go through this cave and you will find a meadow of gold, cross this meadow and you will find yourselves back at the palace. Now go!" The old man was almost shouting. "You must leave this place before it is too late."

"What do you mean?" asked Luna.

"If you are here when the sun goes down, then you can never leave this place." The old man's voice quivered with a sense of foreboding.

"But it is still morning," Solis said. "We arrived here no more than an hour ago."

"That is what you think," the old man said, "but time runs differently here. It is nearly sundown and you only have minutes to get past the end of the road or you will be here forever."

That was the last straw. Solis and Princess Luna ran outside and into the street, they turned and started running back the same way they had come into the town - but they stopped when they saw what awaited them.

A pack of vicious-looking coyotes stood at the end of the road, seemingly eager to tear them both to shreds.

Chapter 8
The Bird

The coyotes had seen them and started to run toward them.

Princess Luna was trembling in fear when she turned to Solis. "What do we do now?"

Solis looked at her. "We go the other way."

Just then the old man stepped out on to the porch of the saloon and yelled, "What are you still doing here? Run, you fools, run!"

Solis and Luna turned and started running as fast as they could.

"We have to run faster, Luna," Solis panted. "The coyotes are getting closer."

The coyotes were now just steps behind them. The sun was starting to set and they were almost there, it was going to be close. Just as the sun set, they jumped and landed outside of the ghost town. They looked at each other and then looked back at the ghost town just in time to see it disappear.

"That was close," said Luna.

"Yeah, a little too close," Solis said.

Then they heard something behind them. They turned around and behind them was a pack of coyotes. One of the coyotes stepped forward and Luna noticed that he was limping a little bit.

"Solis, I think this one is hurt. We should help him," Luna said.

"I think you are right," Solis said.

Just then the coyote sat down in front of Luna and lifted up his left front paw. Luna kneeled down and examined the coyote's paw. There was a large thorn embedded in it. Luna loved animals and she had this extraordinary skill to sense their energy somehow. She held the coyote's paw and pulled out the thorn. The coyote then licked Luna all over her face, and then to their amazement, the coyote said, "Thank you so much! That thorn has been hurting me for days and I couldn't get it out. We have seen the Valley Man and thought that you could help us, so we followed you. I hope we didn't scare you too much. We must be going now so thank you once again."

"I am so happy they just wanted us to help them," Solis said. "I thought we were going to be eaten but they were really nice. Normally, coyotes can be quite dangerous. And I was so surprised they came straight to you, Luna and that you did not fear them. You have this special way with animals I never encountered with anyone. And they even speak when you are around! Since settling here in Death Valley, I have never met an animal who would actually talk to me!"

"I was just happy that I could help them," Luna replied. "She knew that animals can sense her positive high energy influenced by the elements, but Solis could not, yet.

"I think I know where we are at. This is the ancient lake the old man told us about."

"But Solis, don't you think that this old man looked familiar somehow? I feel like I had seen him before."

"I think you are right," Solis said. "I felt the same but I cannot put a finger on where I know him from." Solis looked around. "Look, there is a large rock out there not too far from here. Maybe we should camp here next to the playa, because it is forbidden to camp on it, and then we will go to see it in the morning. You should know that rock formation is called The Grandstand and it is a monolith.

Early the next morning they made their way out into the ancient lake bed to The Grandstand and it was already starting to get hot.

"We need to get to the mountains before it gets dark," Solis said. "There we can find food and shelter."

The two of them started to walk toward the mountains in the distance, and after a few hours, Princess Luna asked, "How much farther is it going to be? It does not look like we are getting any closer and I need to sit down to rest for a minute."

"Ok," Solis said. "Here, let's sit on these rocks and rest." He smiled with sparkles in his eyes.

As the two of them sat down on the rocks, they noticed that the rocks seemed to shake a little bit.

"Did you feel that?" Luna said.

"Yes, but what could it be?"

Just then the rocks that they were sitting on started to move rather fast.

Luna started to scream, but her scream quickly turned into hysterical laughter. "This is fantastic!"

"I know! If we keep going like this we will get to the mountains in no time at all," Solis said.

"You knew about it Solis! You knew about the moving rocks and you wanted me to get surprised with it here." Luna laughed.

"That was a great idea! You managed to impress me with this stunning miracle of nature. Thank you."

"I am glad you liked it so much, Luna," replied Solis happily. He really hoped that Luna would enjoy all the adventures he wanted her to experience with him on this trip.

The two of them rode the rocks and had an amazing fun time all the way across the ancient lake bed. When they arrived at the foot of the mountain they remembered what the old man said: *follow the Canyon of Marble.*

"We need to find out how we can get to the Canyon of Marble. We should set up our camp next to the entrance of this canyon."

They took a short break and started looking for the canyon. After a while, Luna spotted a most peculiar-looking bird running on the ground instead of flying. It had long legs and a long beak and a big tail. Its plumage was mostly brown with some colorful feathers around its eyes and was tall for a bird; it came up to their knees.

"What sort of bird is this," Luna asked. "I bet this bird knows where the canyon is. Too bad we can't ask it for information."

Just as Luna spoke, the bird stopped and said, "Why not? I can tell you where the canyon is. I am a roadrunner and I have lived around here all my life. So, what canyon are you two looking for?"

Solis was shocked, yet he managed to mutter, "The Canyon of Marble."

"Oooh, yes, I know right where that is," the bird said excitedly. "So when are we going to go there?" The bird was now walking along with them.

"We were going to leave in the morning at first light," Luna said. "Would you like to come with us?"

The bird replied, "I can lead you to the entrance but I am not going in."

"Why not?"

"Because all the people who had entered the cave, they never came back," said the bird.

"That is because they go out of the cave at the other end of the canyon," said Solis.

"Oh, I did not think of that. Well, in that case I will go with you as far as the cave, but I will go no further than that," replied the bird.

After a few hours of walking, they arrived at the mouth of a canyon. The bird said, "Here, this is the canyon that you are looking for, the Marble Canyon. I told you I could show you where it is."

"Yes, this appears to be the right one," Solis said. They stood there gazing at the mouth of the canyon, wondering if they'd actually ever get out.

Chapter 9

The Canyon of Marble

"We will make camp here for the night and get a fresh start in the morning at sunrise," Solis said. "We need to find water and food for tonight and take with us into the canyon. Luna, maybe you can take this bird to get some water? I will get us some food."

That night, the three of them sat around the campfire and had a wonderful time telling one another stories of home and their adventures of travelling.

Luna also asked the bird, "Why have you not introduced yourself to us yet? We still do not know your name."

The bird revealed his secret to them: "I did not because I have no name."

Luna felt sad. "Do you mind if we give you a name?"

The Bird was more than curious to know what they were going to name him and he sung a melody, which expressed his excitement to have a name. During his singing, Luna and Solis agreed on his name, and once the bird finished his beautiful singing, Luna said, "From now on you will be called Kiko."

The bird could be not happier and said, "I love this name. I am Kiko Kiko Kiko! In our bird culture, we do not give names but we use sounds to recognize each other."

As much as I know about Death Valley, I never heard about talking birds here. "This is just one of a new things of Death Valley I have been discovering with you Luna on our adventure here together" said Solis. Luna looked at him smiling and said: "What an exciting adventure we are having and it is not over yet."

Kiko said, "I want to sing you a song that my mom always sang to me to help me sleep."

He started to sing, and it was so beautiful that Solis and Princess Luna fell asleep right away. His song sounded like a mysterious lullaby, and soon they were all dreaming of happy times.

They woke up early the next morning at the mouth of the canyon, ready to start their journey. Luna, however, noticed that Kiko was still sleeping.

"I better go and wake up our new friend. It is strange he is still asleep when he, as a bird, should be the first to wake up," said Luna. As she reached down and started to shake Kiko to wake him up, she noticed that he felt unusually cold.

"Solis, come quick! I think there is something wrong with Kiko. He is very cold and I am worried that something bad might have happened to him during the night."

Just then Kiko jumped up and was ready to go. Luna looked at him, still worried. "Are you feeling okay, Kiko? You felt so cold."

Kiko replied running around: "Oh yes, I am feeling great and ready for our adventure. You see, us roadrunners can lower our body temperature slightly, going into a slight torpor during the cold desert nights to help us save our energy. To warm myself up during the day, I run fast like now, exposing dark patches of skin on my back to the sun. It is kind of a thermoregulation process."

"Wow! Nature thought about everything. It just scared me when I saw you still asleep and cold."

"Guys," Solis said. "This is all fascinating, but we need to get on our way so we can make it while it is sunny. Look! There is the entry to the canyon. Let's go!"

This canyon was very beautiful with high walls and narrow pathways; it was a wonder of nature. The walls appeared to be made of marble, and the pathway was covered with little black rocks. It was almost as though someone had put them there, but the reality was they had been brought down the mountain and through the canyon by floods in the past. As they were walking, Solis noticed that the further they got into the canyon, the worse the weather became. He had a sense that something very bad might happen.

Chapter 10
The Dry Falls

After travelling for a few miles or so, they noticed that the weather had become cold and dark clouds were rolling overhead. A wind howled through the canyon that sounded like the screams of a ghost.

"I think we need to hurry up a little bit," Solis said after a while. "I would hate to be in this canyon if it was to rain."

"How much further until we get to the dry falls?" Princess Luna asked. "I think I just felt a rain drop."

"Yeah, me too," Kiko chirped. Just then the rain started to pour down in big fat drops.

"We have to run and try to make it to the Dry Falls," Solis said, "or we will drown if this canyon gets flooded with water."

The three of them took off running like their lives depended on it. Before they knew it, the water was starting to rise, and it was already up to their shins. Kiko was riding on Solis's shoulder. They could see it now, the dry falls, but with one problem: the falls were no longer dry.

"Now what are we going to do?" Luna asked.

"We will have to climb behind the waterfall and get into the cave," replied Solis.

They reached the dry falls and started to climb. The water was coming down increasingly harder every moment. It was getting difficult to hold on to the rocks to climb with all the water pouring on them.

"Oh no," Princess Luna yelled, screaming through the torrent of water. "I can't hold on. It's washing me away!"

Solis looked at her with a gleam in his eye. There's no way he would let anything bad to happen to his beautiful princess. With all his strength, he reached out to her through the water - but caught nothing but air.

Chapter 11
The Mysterious Cave

Thankfully, Princess Luna had seen Solis' arm and grabbed at it just before the water washed her away.

Through sheer force of will, they kept climbing.

Finally they reached the ledge and managed to pull themselves into the opening of the cave.

"That was close," Kiko huffed. "We almost got washed away! It looks like I will be going with you two now through the cave."

As they started walking into the cave they noticed that there were some old mining equipment next to the wall, things like a pick, shovel, a mining hat, a few lanterns, and a box of matches.

"These lanterns will be of good use," Solid said.

They lit the lanterns and saw that there was a note tucked next to the mining hat that read, "For all who find themselves here, turn back and do not enter. But if you must continue on, be warned of the dark and do not let your light go out. May these items help you on your journey through the mountain, and may you reach the meadow on the other side unscathed."

Suddenly there was a strong gust of wind that blew out the lanterns. Then a flash of bright light. The next thing that they saw was that they were no longer in the cave, but in a large room with an old man playing an old pipe organ, and next to the old Man was a pack mule. Solis looked over at Luna and saw something that surprised him:

"Luna, what happened to your hair? It is sticking up like a lion's mane. It looks so funny. Let me help you fix it. There is a mirror over there on the desk, come and see yourself."

Luna walked over and looked into the mirror and panicked.

"I will never be able to comb through this mess of hair," she said very unhappily. Just then a comb flew out of the desk and started to comb her hair, it made short work of the task and had her hair looking great again.

Then the comb said, "We cannot allow our guests to feel unhappy here," and it suddenly disappeared. At this moment they heard a voice that said, "Welcome, our new guests."

Luna and Solis turned around. The room was fancifully decorated and the old man was well groomed and a bit on the large side.

"What was that with the comb and where are we?" Luna's voice was tinged with worry. "What happened? Who are you? What is this place?"

"Please calm down, there is no need to panic," the old man said. "I just thought that you could use some help with your hair, so I had the comb help you out a little bit. Pardon my manners, my name is Scotty and you are in my castle that my dear friends have built here in Death Valley. Walk with me and I will explain everything to you."

"Yes, it was a big help from your magic comb," Luna said, calming down. "Thanks to both of you. My hair is beautiful again. It would take me much longer to get my hair back to its normal shape."

The three of them walked through the old mansion that Scotty so fondly referred to as his castle. It was an old Spanish-style house that was rather large and had stables for horses, a courtyard and even a swimming pool.

"How did we end up here," Solis asked.

"Well, you see, the cave that you went into was not only a cave but it was also one of the hidden entry ways to my gold mine. I put those lanterns and other things there for someone to use if they need to get through my mine. It can be a dangerous place and I used some very old magic to bring anyone that picked up those lanterns here to me. I need to warn you that there are some dangers in that cave. There is a large snake inside and he is not to be trusted. Also, you'll find all the things that crawl and slither you can imagine."

As Solis and Scotty talked and walked through the castle, Scotty's mule joined them. He had his feet ornamented with real diamonds which Scotty bought for him. The mule looked extravagant with the shining diamonds on his feet.

"My name is Slim," the mule said. "I hope you don't mind if I ask you to dance with me?" And before Luna could even answer, he started to dance with her.

Luna was having a great time dancing from room to room with Slim, with Scotty and Solis following them behind. As they neared one of the last rooms, Solis could hear what sounded like wind howling from under the door.

"What is in that room?" Solis asked.

"That is one of the entries to my mine. There is always a wonderfully scented wind coming out of it that smells like vanilla," said Scotty.

Luna had caught up with them and said, "Your place is amazing."

"Oh, well, you can come and see my castle another day but for now I must send you back to finish your journey and get back

to the palace. Remember the breeze will always blow from the correct path," said Scotty as he faded away right before their eyes. Then the wind howling from under the door got louder and louder and blew the door right off, and then there was a bright flash of light.

The next thing they knew was that they were back in the cave with the lanterns in hand and Kiko saying, "Are you two ready? Let's go. Let's go."

Solis and Luna just looked at each other with astonishment.

"Did that really just happen?" asked Luna.

"I think it did. We just met Death Valley Scotty. He was an old timer that lived here many years ago. He was a performer and came here to do prospecting. He was also a bit of a con man and told everyone that he had a very rich gold mine in order to get investors give him money. But the creepy thing is, he has been dead for a long time now. For some unknown reason, I think we went back to the past then bounced back to the present. How was it possible?"

"What are you both talking about?" asked Kiko. "You were here all the time. Who's Scotty?"

"You won't believe what happened to us, Kiko," Luna said excitedly. "We time travelled somehow. We went back to the past for a moment, then quickly got back to the present. You didn't notice it?"

"You are pulling my leg. A good joke, you two! You were here all the time next to me."

The two of them just looked at each other for a minute and then Luna said, "We should gather anything that would be helpful and get going. This cave seems scary."

"That sounds like a good idea to me. Let's go," replied Solis.

Solis and Luna picked up the items and started on their way into the cave.

Luna said, "Did you feel that?"

"Yes," Solis said, "I felt a cold chill run down my spine like this cave is hiding something, like it has a secret that it doesn't want us to know."

The three of them started on their way, going deeper into the cave. The sound of the waterfall was all but gone now. The soft flickering glow of the lanterns lit the path of the cave ever so gently.

"This is not so bad," Solis said, "I wonder how far it is to the other side."

After a few more minutes, they started to notice that the floor of the cave had changed a little bit, it was now making crunching sounds with every step and now and then they could see a little movement on the cave walls if the light was on it.

"What could this be on the ground," Solis said, "making these crunching sounds?"

He lowered his lantern, and when he did they saw the floor of the cave was covered with scorpions and spiders! They all surrounded them, like some hideous carpet of creepy crawlies.

Luna screamed, her shrieks echoing throughout the dark, cavernous space.

Chapter 12
The Snake Pit

Solis urged them on. "We need to keep moving. We should not stop!"

"Can we move faster?" Princess Luna said. "I want to get out of here." Luna was deathly afraid of insects and arachnids. Where she was from there were no such things and she was very scared.

"But this is true paradise," Kiko exclaimed. "Sooooo much fooood! So delightful. I love to eat scorpions and spiders." Kiko caught a scorpion and started to eat it.

"Solis, let's go as fast as we can from here," Luna said. "Let Kiko stay and let him enjoy his meal. He can catch up with us quickly later."

"Oh, yeees, there is no rush for me. I will catch up with you once I've had my fill. Really, do not worry about me, as you know I can run fast!" replied Kiko happily, a scorpion struggling in his beak. Luna could not really understand how anyone can eat scorpions and spiders, and this very much surprised her.

By this point, they were almost at a run trying to get through the cave, and away from all the creepy crawlies. After a few minutes, they noticed that the crunching sound had ceased. They stopped and again lowered the lantern to see the ground, and to their relief it was just rocks and dirt once again.

"Thank goodness, we made it past all that," Solis panted. "I hope it is easy the rest of the way."

Kiko also materialized from nowhere with a big smile on his face, screaming happily, "I am here! I am here now. I told you I would reach you faster than you thought. I can run 30 kilometres per hour."

"You made it, Kiko," Solis said. "You are great! But now let's go. We still have a long way to go."

The three of them continued on for what seemed like hours when all of a sudden they came across a split in the tunnel.

"Which way do we go?" Princess Luna's voice quivered with apprehension. "How do we know which is the way out?"

"I am not sure," Solis replied, "but there is only one way to find out. Let's go left."

Just as they were starting to go down the left tunnel, they heard a hiss and it sssssssaid, "Don't go that way." They stopped and looked around.

"Is someone there? Come out and show yourself, step into the light," Solis called out. Just then the lantern started to flicker and went out. The cave was again dark as a moonless night. And at this moment Luna's hair begun to glow with a million stars.

"Ok, but you are not going to like it," the voice said.

Just then a rather large snake slithered into the light, rising up from the darkness, looking Solis straight in the eye. This snake had heavy sand-colored scales with a spotted dark brown pattern on its back, and it had a rattle at the end of its tail. It also had two little horns on the end of its nose.

The snake spoke, "Don't go that way."

Solis was astonished, yet he managed to ask, "Well, where does this path go?"

"I cannot tell you that," the snake hissed, "but all I can *sssssssay* is that one path leads out of the cave and into the meadow and the other path leads to a bottomless*sss* pit and a horrible death."

"Well, how do we know which path to take then?" Luna said.

"You have to make this choice for yourselves," the snake said. "But choose wisely for once you start down a path, there is no turning back."

Solis and the princess and Kiko looked at one another for a minute and then they felt a slight bit of wind coming from the tunnel on the right.

"I think we should go right," Solis said. "Did you feel that? The wind coming from the right tunnel? That means there is an opening that way and it is not too far either."

The three of them started to walk down the tunnel on the right, then they heard a little bit of a rumble and it grew louder and louder, so they started to run. They stopped and looked back just on time to see the walls and roof cave in and block the way back to where they had just come from.

Just then the snake appeared again right in front of them. "I *sssssee* you have made your choice on which way you want to go. Shall we *sssssssee* if you have chosen correctly?"

Solis and Princess Luna continued down the path and to their surprise it seemed to be easy going.

Kiko was still riding on Solis's shoulder and the snake was just slithering behind them, keeping its distance. "I can eat this snake, you know I can," Kiko whispered to Solis. "I would be delighted, even though my tummy's full from eating scorpions and spiders. This snake annoys me so much."

"Yes, Kiko, I know that you eat snakes but this one is a little bit too big, even for you."

"I don't like this," Princess Luna said. "This is too easy. Something is wrong, and the snake is creeping me out just following us, like it is waiting for something to happen."

"I know," Solis said. "I get the same feeling."

"I think I see something up ahead," Kiko said. "It looks like a big hole in the path."

Soon the three of them were close enough to see what it was, and Kiko was right. It was a large pit, probably several metres in diametre. This pit, however, was not truly bottomless; it was full of snakes just waiting for their next meal to come along. The snake that was following them had disappeared and was nowhere to be seen.

"Do you think we can jump across it?" Solis asked the princess.

"I do not think we have another way," Princess Luna said, taking a deep breath. "We really have to jump."

"Look, there are some plant roots jutting out of the ceiling," Kiko said, pointing up. "If we can climb along the wall over to that ledge, then we can reach those roots and swing the rest of the way across."

"That is a brilliant idea, Kiko," Solis said.

"I will go first to make sure that it is possible, and then when I get across you two can follow," Solis said to Luna and Kiko.

Solis climbed the wall and made it to the ledge without a hitch. Then he grabbed what looked to be a sturdy root and gave it a few good tugs just to be sure that it was going to hold.

"Here goes nothing," Solis said, then he jumped off the ledge, swinging toward the other side of the pit. Underneath him, hundreds of snakes slithered and hissed and awaited his fall. Something snapped and Luna screamed.

Chapter 13
The Escape

The snapping sound came from the vine as Solis let go of it, swinging deftly to the other side of the pit.

"Climb to that ledge, you can make it," he yelled back to his companions. "You should have no problem."

Luna started climbing the wall to get over to the ledge. When she got there, the big snake appeared again and slithered towards her.

"Hurry, Luna, the snake is coming to get us," screamed Kiko.

Luna grabbed a root. Taking a deep breath, she jumped from the ledge and was swinging through the air to the other side of the pit when she felt the root start to break.

"I hope we make it," she said. "We are almost there."

Just then the root snapped and Luna landed on the edge of the pit just enough to grab on the edge, half her body hanging down. She tried to clutch at whatever she could hold on to, yet there was nothing but loose rocks.

She was just about to fall when Solis reached out and grabbed her hand and pulled her toward him. She fell forward right into his arms.

"Thanks," she panted, looking into his eyes. "You just saved my life."

They looked into each other's eyes for a moment and started to lean in to kiss when they heard Kiko say, "That's enough, you two. Besides, I think I can see the way out of here. Look!"

They both looked up and saw that Kiko was right. It was the way out and not that far ahead. They had made it through the cave.

"Let's hurry," Princess Luna said. "I can't wait to be out of here."

The three of them were now running toward the exit. When they got there, they saw the meadow. It was like nothing they had ever seen before.

Chapter 14
The Golden Meadow of Forgetfulness

The meadow stretched out in front of them like a carpet of golden yellow flowers that covered the whole valley floor with an extraordinary beautiful but strong smell, reminding them of the smell of homemade vanilla cookies. The three of them just stood there at the exit of the cave and looked in awe for a few moments.

"Have you ever seen anything so spectacular?" Luna said.

"No, never in my life," replied Solis. "It is another new discovery to me. As though Death Valley is showing me things that no one knows about. But listen, everyone, it will be getting dark soon and we should find somewhere to camp. It's not safe in this cave."

Suddenly, Kiko grabbed a lizard to Luna's surprise and ate it in front of her. "Kiko, I did not know you eat lizards!" screamed Luna. "That was unusually weird and gross." Then she cringed and turned away from the scene.

"I was so hungry and when I saw it, I had to eat it," Kiko said. "It is a very delicious and healthy food for us roadrunners."

"Solis, did you know about this? Did you know that birds eat lizards here?" asked Luna.

Solis laughed. "Oh yes, Luna, that's quite normal for birds here. You will get used to it."

Luna still could not believe what she just saw and asked Kiko, "Will you please do not eat lizards in front of me? Poor lizards. It just does not feel nice seeing you eating them."

Unable to understand Luna's request, Kiko shook his head.

Then Solis said, "Alright, let's look for a nice spot to camp now."

The three of them found a nice little area on the edge of the meadow that had a few trees, and a little stream going through it. There they set up camp for the night, caught some fish, and gathered some mesquite beans and made them that wonderful sweet drink again, the same as Timbosha had prepared before.

Luna was gathering firewood and some rocks to make a bonfire when something most unexpected happened. She picked up what she thought was a rock, which suddenly spoke. "Excuse me, but can you please put me down? I am afraid of heights and I don't like to be picked up."

Luna was so startled; she looked at the rock she had just picked up and noticed that it now had legs and a head.

"Be careful, don't drop me," the rock said.

"What are you?" Luna asked.

"I am a desert tortoise and I live here in this meadow because all of the nice flowers and grasses here are very good to eat," said the tortoise.

Luna set the tortoise back on the ground and asked, "What is your name?"

"My name is Tortoise Tarda. It was very nice to meet you. Now, if you don't mind I must be on my way back home."

"Well, do you want to come and join us for dinner?"

"No, us tortoises are really creatures of habit and don't like to disturb our routine. Also I have a very well-established home where I have everything I need: food, water and mineral resources," Tortoise Tarda said. "And I am supposed to be home now. So, if you don't mind I will be on my way."

Luna rushed back to the camp and told Solis all about her strange encounter with the tortoise and how exciting it was to see all these new and amazing things here. Solis said, "You met another animal – actually a reptile who can talk? Did you know that there are turtles and tortoises, they both come from the order Testudines. The major difference between them is that tortoise will live on land, and can even live in some really dry hot climates whereas turtles will live mostly in and around water. We have tortoises in Death Valley since there is not much water there. You were lucky to meet tortoise Tarda because they are so rarely seen here, but most sightings are after a good rain. Also we are so lucky we can experience the meadow full of flowers now too."

Luna was so surprised by Solis's knowledge of the subject and just replied:

"The nature here amazes me so much. I did not expect to see so much of wonderful wildlife in a place called Death Valley. I have to admit that when I first heard the name Death Valley I thought it was just going to be a lifeless desert. I was so mistaken. There are quite many plants and animals here. More than where I come from. But also Death Valley reminds me little on my home because it has this kind of a similar lunar landscape. Maybe one day I tell you more about it or I could show you if you come to visit me. I think you would be amazed too but in a different way."

Kiko was just listening to their conversation. Then the three of them ate supper while sitting by the nice fire, enjoying the vanilla cookie smell of the meadow around them. Luna still could not stop thinking about Kiko eating the poor lizard. Kiko felt it and decided to sing his beautiful melodies to make Luna feel better. Soon they were fast asleep and dreaming of home and their adventures.

The sun rose like every other morning, and yet today seemed to be different. Today, when the three of them awoken, there was no sense of danger and no sense of urgency.

They got up and sat in the camp, talking about the journey they have had so far. There was something unique about this meadow and all the flowers that grew here. These flowers were not as innocent as they appeared. They have a special poison that was carried by the wind and hidden by the flowers' sweet smell. This sweet poison makes who ever smells it lose all of their worries and all their thoughts of going home and so they stay there in the meadow until it is too late.

As they started to walk through the meadow, Luna said, "Can we just stay for a few more hours? My feet hurt and I am still a little bit tired."

Solis stopped and looked at her for a second and said, "Well, we do have a nice place to camp that has all we need and this beautiful meadow to look at with the wonderful smell of the flowers wafting in the breeze. So, sure, let's stay for one more day."

The problem was that it was not just one more day. Each morning, the three of them would wake up, get ready to go back home, and start walking through the meadow and find some reason that they had to stay just one more day. It was indeed the Golden Meadow of Forgetfulness.

This went on for about a week, until one morning when they woke up to find a surprise visitor in their camp, an old man with long gray hair, mustache and a beard. The same one as they met before in the ghost town.

"You again," said Solis. "Who are you? What is your name?"

"I don't know," said the old man. "I have been out here for so long I can't remember my name. All that does not matter, I have come to warn you about this place and the danger you are in."

"What danger?" Luna asked skeptically, "This place is peaceful and we have everything we need right here."

"Yes, yes, don't you see that? *That* is the danger. You are already starting to forget about your thoughts of going home. That is what this meadow does, it wants you to stay, and it wants you to be here until it is too late for you to go. You must leave this place before it is too late."

Solis thought about the old man's words. He turned to Princess Luna. "You know what? I think he is right. Every day, we have been coming up with a reason to stay here longer and we have been here for over a week now. We need to get back home and we need to go today."

Luna said, "But it is so lovely here. Can we not just stay one or two days longer please? I love this meadow and the vanilla smell. I do not feel like leaving this place yet."

"We need to leave today Luna," said Solis. "Let's get ready now, please. I like this place a lot, too, as you do but I want us all to be safe. Please, let's leave now."

"I am ready," said Kiko in sing-song.

"We should leave now," said Solis, then he turned around, surprising all of them. "I think I recognize you from the saloon painting now. Oh oh oh – you must be my lost great grandfather

named Helios. Am I crazy to think that? Are you my great grandpa?"

"Actually, I believe I am, but I cannot remember it exactly, Solis. That's why I am here to help you to get back home safely. I do not want you to share the same fate as mine!"

Solis tried to give Helios a hug but he could not feel anything. He was very curious about his great grandpa's history, so he asked him, "Great Grandpa, what happened to you? Why did you vanish all those years ago?"

Grandpa Helios replied with tears in his eyes. "I tried to save some visitors, which I succeeded in doing, but then a heavy storm came and the flood washed me through the canyon. I woke up in the ghost town. I noticed something was different with me. I could no longer feel my body, I could not pick up anything, and I could not leave this place anymore. I became a ghost."

Solis could not believe the story. "There are so many questions I would like to ask you. Is there any chance I can get you out of here? Can I help you somehow? Is there anything I can do for you? Am I going to see you again?"

"We will meet another day, Solis, but now you all have to go!" replied Helios.

They all quickly said goodbye and Kiko sung a beautiful heart-touching good-bye song. Then the three of them gathered some food and water and started on their way. This time they were determined to make it across the meadow and back home.

Chapter 15
The Trek Home

Solis said to Luna, "If you start to feel like you want to stay here, just tell me a story of something that you like or miss about your home, and I will do the same if I feel like I want to stay."

The three of them continued walking and telling stories to one another about their lives, and homes, and all the things they missed and wanted to see again. They got to know each other very well by doing this, and most importantly, they made it across the meadow.

"There it is," Luna screamed with excitement. "Death Valley and the palace. We are almost there. We finally made it."

"We should be there in an hour or so," Solis said.

When they arrived at the palace, Luna was greeted by all her friends. They have been worried and were so happy to see her again. She started to tell them all about the adventures she had just experienced.

Solis and Kiko just kind of fell into the background with all the excitement, so they decided to go. After all, Luna was a princess, and Solis was just a valley man and whatever he was thinking could never work.

When Solis got outside of the palace, he sat down on the steps and said, "At least, we made it back, right Kiko?"

Just then he heard the door open behind him. It was Princess Luna.

"You weren't planning on leaving, were you? I kind of like having you around," said the princess.

Solis looked at her and said, "I need to pick up Badaboo but before I go, I want to ask you Luna how is this going to work? You are a princess and I am just a valley man."

Princess Luna smiled and said, "None of those things matter. It doesn't matter if you are rich, or poor, or a prince, or a valley man. We have had a great adventure together and I have found something really very special on our journey. I found the person I love, the person I want to spend the rest of my life with, and the one I want to have many more adventures with, and that is you, Solis."

Solis pulled her close and gave her a big kiss. "I love you, my Luna, and I can't wait to see what further adventures await us." He paused, looking intently into her eyes. "Have you ever heard of a place called the Grand Canyon?"

And their adventures never end…

BIGHORN
SHEEP

MULE

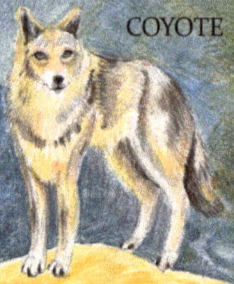
COYOTE

DEATH
VALLEY

TARANTULA

RAVEN

LIZARD

TORTOISE

SCORPION

ROADRUNNER

RATTLESNAKE

JACKRABBIT

KIT FOX

KANGAROO
RAT

Death Valley Facts

- Death Valley was made a National Monument in 1933 and was made a National Park in 1994.

- Death Valley National park is a little more than 3.4 million acres, Death Valley National Park is the largest national park in the Lower 48.

- Death Valley is in 2 Different States: California and Nevada.

- The highest recorded temperature in the world was recorded in Death Valley's Furnace Creek at 134 Fahrenheit (56,6 Celsius degrees) in July, 1913.

- Death Valley is the driest place in the country. In 1929, there was not a single drop of rain recorded in Death Valley.

- Death Valley has the country's lowest point, this is Badwater Basin, 282 feet below sea level (86 meters below sea level), and due to seismic activity it is getting lower every year.

- Death Valleys highest peak is Telescope peak, 11049 feet about sea level (3367,7 m about sea level), it is only 15 miles (24 km) from the parks lowest point.

☞ Death Valley National Park has more than:

- 1000 species of plants (including 50 that are found nowhere else in the world)
- 300 species of birds.
- 51 species of mammals (including bighorn sheep and mountain lions)
- 36 species of reptiles and a handful of amphibian and fish species (including the pupfish which some are only found here in Death Valley).

☞ Death Valley Archaeologists have found evidence of human presence in Death Valley that dates back at least 9,000 years!

☞ The Timbisha Shoshone Native American Tribe has in habited Death Valley for the past 1,000 years.

☞ The Palm Trees in Death Valley are not native to the park, they have been introduced by man to the area mostly used to grow dates.

☞ Dozens of scenes from the Star Wars movies have been filmed in Death Valley. Very exciting!

☞ Death Valley has thousands of old mines and dozens of old ghost towns where the miners once lived.

☞ Rhyolite is one of the most popular ghost town near the Eastern edge of Death Valley.

☞ Just outside of Rhyolite there is an outdoor sculpture park called the Goldwell Open Air Museum. It is a nonprofit museum which was organised in 2000 after the death of an Polish-Belgian artist Albert Szukalski who was best known as the sculptor of works that the artist termed "ghosts".

He travelled to Nevada desert in year 1984 to create "The Last Supper" sculpture which it is considered to be the centerpiece of the Goldwell Open Air Museum.

☞ The sculpture, The Last Supper, consists of ghostly life-sized white forms arranged as in the painting The Last Supper by Leonardo da Vinci. Szukalski molded his shapes by draping plaster-soaked burlap over live models until the plaster dried enough to stand on its own. In the same year, using the same techniques, Szukalski also created Ghost Rider, a plaster figure preparing to mount a bicycle.

☞ Death Valley was included as a UNESCO site in 1984 as a principle feature of its Mojave and Colorado Deserts biosphere reserve.

Book Quiz

Questions

1. *What animal is the only animal in the park that is not of need to drink water?*
   (a) kit fox
   (b) Kangaroo rat
   (c) Tortoise

2. *What kind of animal is Kiko?*
   (a) Raven
   (b) Roadrunner
   (c) Tarantula

3. *What is the other name for the sea of sand?*
   (a) Mesquite flat sand dunes
   (b) Racetrack
   (c) Zabriskie Point

4. *What kind of animal is Death Valley Scotty's favorite pet?*
    (a) Horse
    (b) Mule
    (c) Snake

5. *What kind of reptiles live in Death Valley?*
    (a) Snakes
    (b) Lizards
    (c) Turtles

6. *What is the lowest point in the park?*
    (a) The Sand Dunes
    (b) The barren salt flats also known as bad water basin
    (c) Furnace Creek Inn

7. *What is the highest point in the park?*
    (a) Telescope peak
    (b) Mosaic Canyon
    (c) Scotty's Castle

8. *Does the park have any fish?*
    (a) No, there are no fish
    (b) Yes, it is the pupfish

9. *What is the other name for the area of moving rocks called in the book ancient lake bed?*
    (a) The running rocks
    (b) The racetrack
    (c) The Big Bear Rock

10. *What are the two places which does not exist in Death Valley but are mentioned in the book?*
    (a) The Oasis
    (b) The Cave
    (c) The Marble Canyon

11. *What kind of flower is the most common during a bloom in Death Valley and was in the Meadow of Forgetfulness?*
    (a) Desert gold
    (b) Desert rose
    (c) Desert five spot

12. *Does the sand beast really exist in Death Valley?*
    (a) Yes
    (b) No

13. *Which two states is Death Valley National Park in?*
    (a) California and Nevada
    (b) California and Arizona
    (c) California and New York

14. *What is the hottest temperature recorded in Death Valley?*
    (a) 146 Farenheit
    (b) 180 Farenheit
    (c) 134 Farenheit

15. *How big is Death Valley National Park?*
    (a) 3.4 million acres
    (b) 1.5 million acres

(c) 527 thousands acres

16. *When did Death Valley become a National Park?*
    (a) 1933
    (b) 1894
    (c) 1994

17. *What is the name of the Native American tribe that lives in Death Valley?*
    (a) The Navajo
    (b) The Timbisha Shoshone
    (c) The *Pawnee*

18. *What can you take as a souvenir from National Parks:*
    (a) rocks
    (b) plants
    (c) animals
    (d) none *of the above*

19. *What should you always do visiting National Park:*
    (a) always clean up after yourself and be sure all your trash goes to the proper location
    (b) always be respectful of other guests
    (c) always be sure to keep safe distance from the wildlife
    (d) all of the above

All the answers will be posted on our Facebook *Page:*

The Princess and the Valley Man
http://bit.ly/2rdzfv

Authors

Dorota Kluza was born on September 27, 1976 in Lubin. She graduated with two masters degrees in law at the Adam Mickiewicz University in Poznań as well as at the European University Viadrina in Frankfurt (Oder). She is a world traveler, writer, actress, model, and translator. She speaks Polish as her native tongue, then also English, German, Spanish and some Russian as well. Privately, she is passionate about traveling, music, dancing, cinema as well extreme sports and scuba diving. The magic of connecting with nature inspired her to create the tale of The Princess and the Valley Man. She hopes the story will transport the readers to another time and place. Her life motto is: Sky has no limits.

Evan Williams was born and raised in a small town called Tremonton in Northern Utah but living in Los Angeles now. He served in the United States Army for nearly 9 years where he had the opportunity to travel all over Europe and the Middle East. Later on he moved to Southern Utah and attended the Southern Utah university where he earned a bachelor degree in national resource management. During and after his studies he worked for the National Park Service as a Park Ranger at The Grand Canyon and Death Valley national parks. His Park Ranger experience and love for traveling, adventure, and the great outdoors gave him inspiration to write the tales of The Princess and the Valley Man.

Illustrator:

Małgorzata   Barcikowska-Nazarczuk was born in 1975 in Malbork and living in Warsaw now. She graduated from the State Secondary School of Fine Arts in Olsztyn and then the Academy of Fine Arts in Gdańsk. Her works are admired in Poland and abroad. She creates new projects, and her exhibitions and artistic shows are highly appreciated. The greatest inspirations for the artist are two daughters, nature and dreams. She loves reading, designing, cooking and traveling. Drawing illustrations for books is one of her greatest childhood dreams.

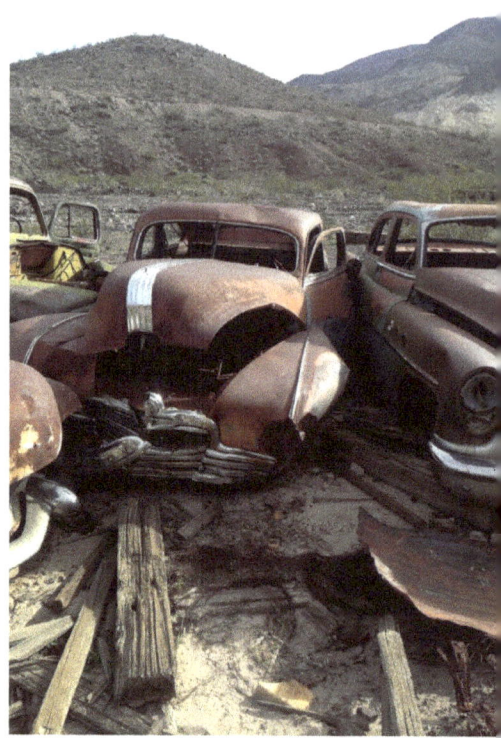

Abandoned cars somewhere in Death Valley

www.ingramcontent.com/pod-product-compliance
Lightning Source LLC
Chambersburg PA
CBHW051211090426
42740CB00022B/3468